Unusual Animals

Giant Anteater

Sara Antill

WINDMILL
BOOKS

New York

Published in 2011 by Windmill Books, LLC
303 Park Avenue South, Suite # 1280, New York, NY 10010-3657

First Edition

CREDITS:
Author: Sara Antill
Edited by: Jennifer Way
Designed by: Brian Garvey

Photo Credits: Cover, p. 22 (top) © www.iStockphoto.com/Eric Isselée; cover background © www.iStockphoto.com/Michal Krakowiak; p. 4–5 © www.iStockphoto.com/Mike Brown; pp. 5 (inset), 6 (top), 20 Shutterstock.com; p. 6 (bottom) Tom Fowlks/Getty Images; p. 7 © www.iStockphoto.com/Warwick Lister-Kaye; p. 8 Joel Sartore/Getty Images; p. 9 © www.iStockphoto.com/Sondra Paulson; pp. 10, 14 © SuperStock/age fotostock; p. 11 © Mark Jones/age fotostock; p. 12-13 PHOTO 24/Getty Images; p. 15 (top) © www.iStockphoto.com/fanelie rosier; pp. 15 (bottom), 22 (bottom) © www.iStockphoto.com/Paul Erickson; p. 16-17 Tom Ulrich/Getty Images; p. 18 (inset) © www.iStockphoto.com/Alberto L. Pomares G.; p. 18-19 © Juniors Bildarchiv; p. 21 © FLPA/age fotostock.

Library of Congress Cataloging-in-Publication Data

Antill, Sara.
 Giant anteater / by Sara Antill. — 1st ed.
    p. cm. — (Unusual animals)
 Includes index.
 ISBN 978-1-60754-993-2 (library binding) — ISBN 978-1-61533-001-0 (pbk.) — ISBN 978-1-61533-002-7 (6-pack)
 1. Myrmecophaga—Juvenile literature. I. Title.
 QL737.E24A68 2011
 599.3'14—dc22

2010004433

Manufactured in the United States of America

For more great fiction and nonfiction, go to windmillbooks.com.

CPSIA Compliance Information: Batch # BW2011WM: For Further Information contact Windmill Books, New York, New York at 1-866-478-0556

Table of Contents

Built for One Thing............................... 4

Time to Eat!... 10

Along for the Ride.............................. 18

Inside Story.. 22

Glossary.. 23

Read More... 24

Index.. 24

Web Sites.. 24

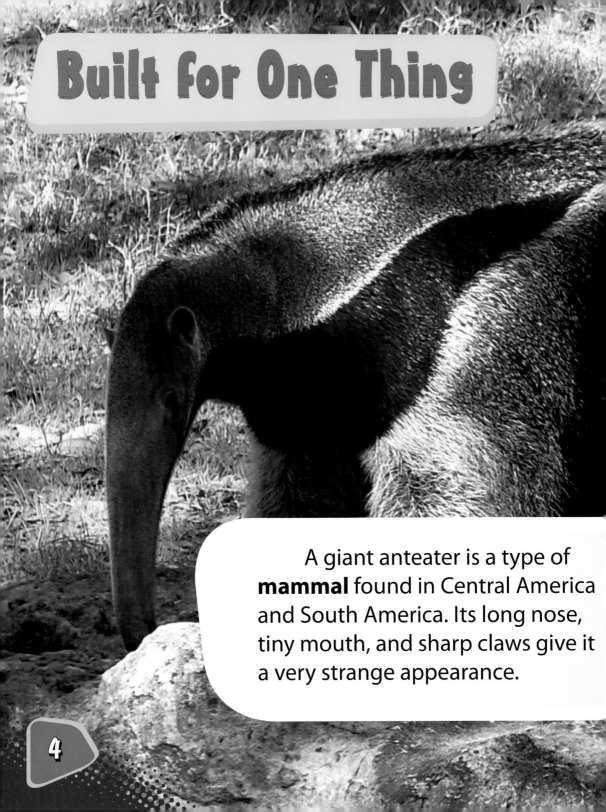

Built for One Thing

A giant anteater is a type of **mammal** found in Central America and South America. Its long nose, tiny mouth, and sharp claws give it a very strange appearance.

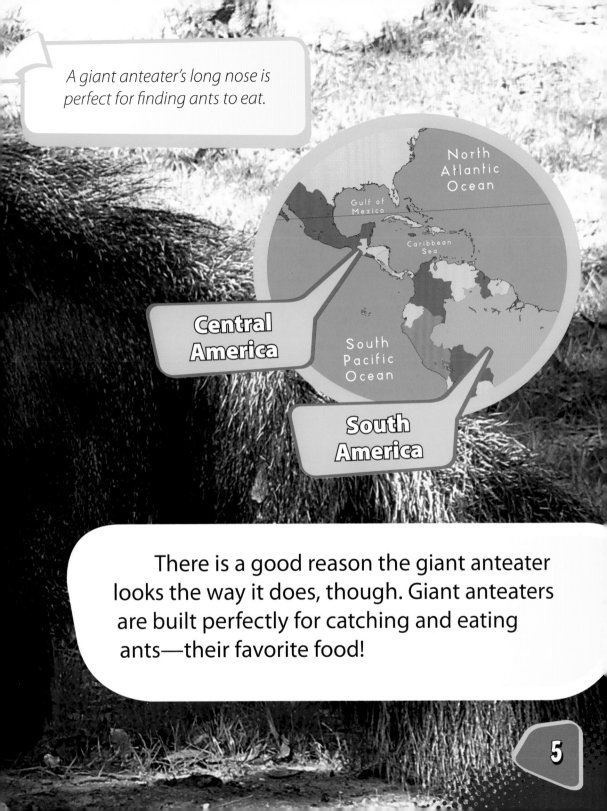

A giant anteater's long nose is perfect for finding ants to eat.

North Atlantic Ocean

Gulf of Mexico

Caribbean Sea

Central America

South Pacific Ocean

South America

There is a good reason the giant anteater looks the way it does, though. Giant anteaters are built perfectly for catching and eating ants—their favorite food!

Many giant anteaters live in warm, wet **rain forests**. A rain forest is an area with many trees and plants.

Rainforests are warm and wet year-round.

Giant anteaters can also live on dry **savannas**, or grasslands. There are fewer trees on savannas. Anteaters will live anywhere where there are lots of insects for them to eat.

This giant anteater lives in a grassland area.

Giant anteaters are the largest type of anteater. An adult can be as long as 7 feet (2.1 m) and can weigh over 100 pounds (45 kg).

A worker in Brazil feeds this young giant anteater.

Giant anteaters are covered with thick hair that feels like straw.

All giant anteaters have a black stripe that reaches from under their nose to the middle of their body. Their coloring helps them blend in with the plants around them.

Three large claws on each front paw help the giant anteater reach its food. It uses these strong claws to rip open an ant or termite hill.

Ants will bite animals that attack their home. Giant anteaters only spend about one minute feeding at each anthill.

Giant anteaters are careful not to destroy an entire anthill when they are feeding. That way, the ants can easily fix their home. Then the anteater can come back to feed there another time!

Tongue

When it's time to eat, the giant anteater's amazing tongue comes in handy. The sticky tongue is more than 2 feet (61 cm) long.

The giant anteater can move its tongue in and out of the anthill 150 to 160 times a minute!

A giant anteater's long, skinny tongue is perfect for catching ants.

Giant anteaters do not have any teeth in their small mouth. Instead, they swallow sand and tiny rocks. In the stomach, these little rocks help to mash up the ants and termites that the anteater has swallowed.

13

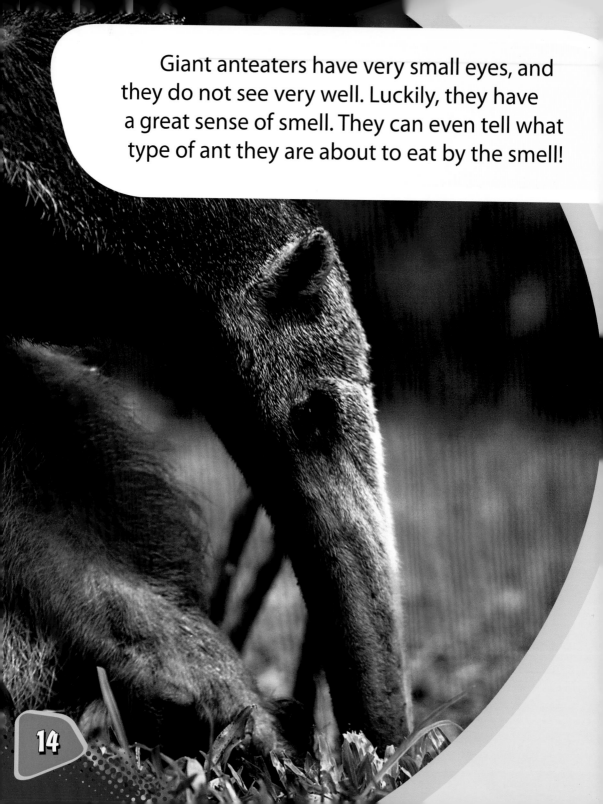

Giant anteaters have very small eyes, and they do not see very well. Luckily, they have a great sense of smell. They can even tell what type of ant they are about to eat by the smell!

A good sense of smell is also useful to avoid **predators**. Big cats like the jaguar and the puma will hunt and kill a giant anteater. An anteater can also defend itself with its sharp claws.

These black ants are just outside their anthill.

Giant anteaters are **solitary** animals. This means they usually live alone. They spend their time wandering from place to place, looking for food. When it is time to sleep, they find a safe place, such as a hollow log.

This giant anteater looks for ants on the grassy plains of Brazil.

Giant anteaters that live closer to people are **nocturnal**. This means they sleep during the day and are active at night.

However, anteaters that live further away from people are **diurnal**. They sleep at night and are active during the day.

Along for the Ride

A female giant anteater will give birth once every 1 or 2 years. Giant anteaters have just one baby at a time. The baby is called a "pup." When the baby is born, it will drink milk from its mother's body, as do all mammals.

Here is a giant anteater pup riding on its mother's back.

A young anteater rides on its mother's back. It will stay with her until it is about 2 years old, or until she has another baby.

In many places in South America, trees are burned down to make way for farms. This destroys the giant anteater's habitat.

Like many animals, giant anteaters are in danger of disappearing from our planet. They are hunted for their **pelts**, and they can be hit by cars when they cross roads. The worst threat to giant anteaters is **habitat destruction**.

When people cut down trees and destroy the rain forest, they are destroying the anteaters' home. Many groups are working together to create **nature reserves.** These are places where giant anteaters and other animals will be safe.

CUIDADO POSSO ATRAVESSA

SINFRA   EDUCAÇÃO AMBIENTAL   M

This sign in Brazil warns drivers to look out for giant anteaters trying to cross the road.

21

Inside Story

Giant anteaters are very good swimmers.

When they are scared, giant anteaters will stand on their two back feet to fight. They use their bushy tail to hold themselves up.

A giant anteater can eat 35,000 ants in one day!

Glossary

DIURNAL (dy-UR-nul) Something that is active during the day.

HABITAT DESTRUCTION (HA-bih-tat dee-STRUK-shun) When someone's home is destroyed.

MAMMAL (MA-mull) A warm-blooded animal that usually gives birth to live young instead of laying eggs.

NATURE RESERVE (NAY-chur ree-zerv) An area set aside for plants and animals to grow where they are safe from people.

NOCTURNAL (nahk-TUR-nul) Something that is active at night.

PELT (PELT) The skin of an animal.

PREDATOR (PREH-da-tur) An animal who hunts another animal for food.

RAIN FOREST (RAYN for-est) An warm, tropical area with lots of trees and a high amount of rain every year.

SAVANNA (suh-VA-nuh) A grassy area with scattered trees.

SOLITARY (SAH-lih-teh-ree) Living alone.

Index

A
ants.............5, 11, 14
C
Central America 5
claws 10, 15
H
hair...........................9
J
jaguar...................15

M
mammal...........5, 18
N
nature reserve 21
P
pelt 20
puma....................15
R
rain forest 6

S
savanna...................7
South America.......5
T
teeth...................... 13
tongue............12-13

Read More

Jenkins, Steve. *Actual Size*. New York: Houghton Mifflin Books for Children, 2004.

Seiple, Samantha and Todd Seiple. *Giant Anteaters*. Minneapolis, MN: Lerner Publishing Group, 2008.

Snedden, Robert. *South America*. Mankato, MN: Capstone Press, 2003.

Web Sites

For Web resources related to the subject of this book, go to: www.windmillbooks.com/weblinks and select this book's title.